Be My Valentine

Valentine's Day Coloring Book

Color Your Heart, Color your Love

Kimberly Harold

Happy Coloring

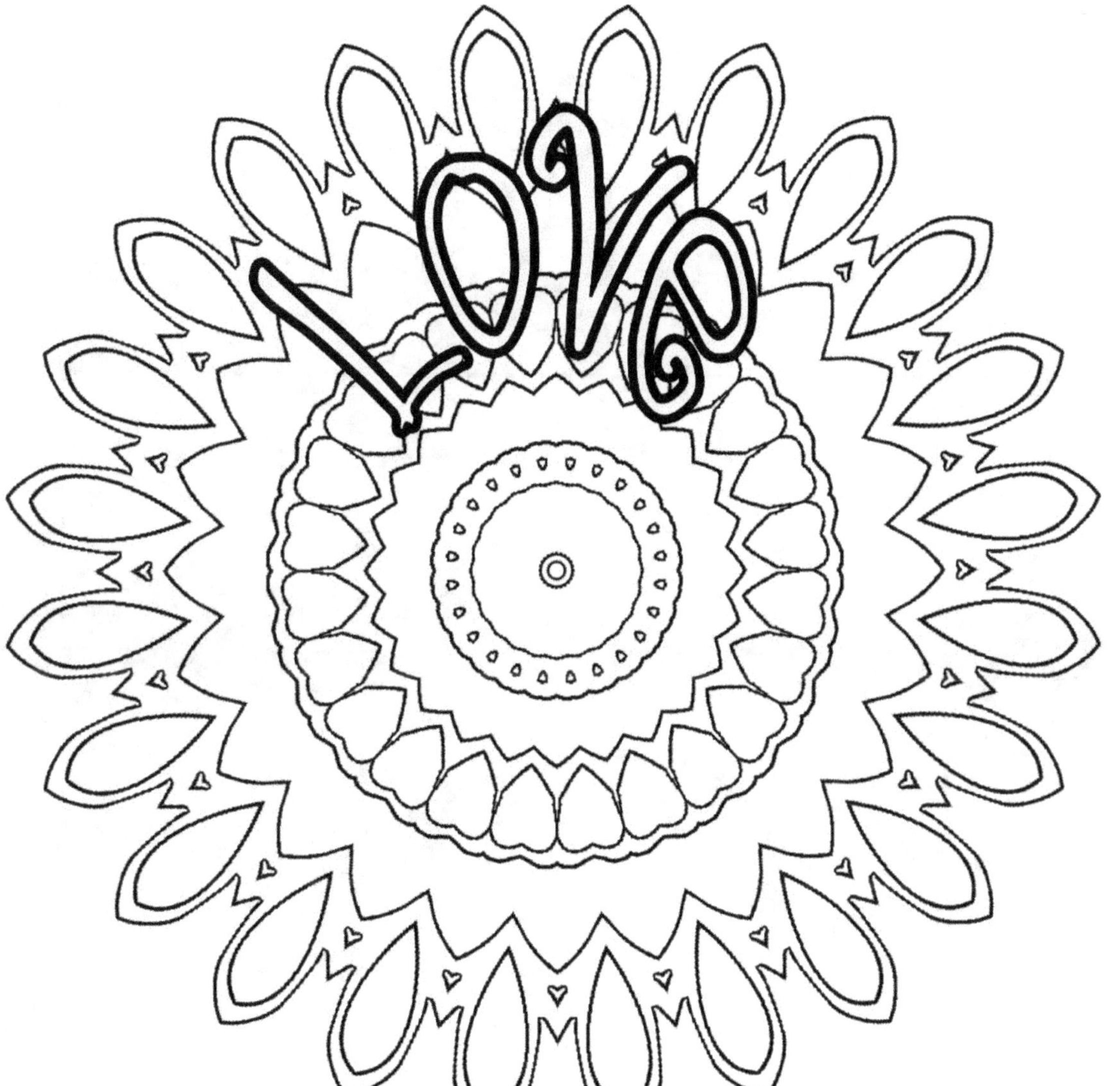
Love

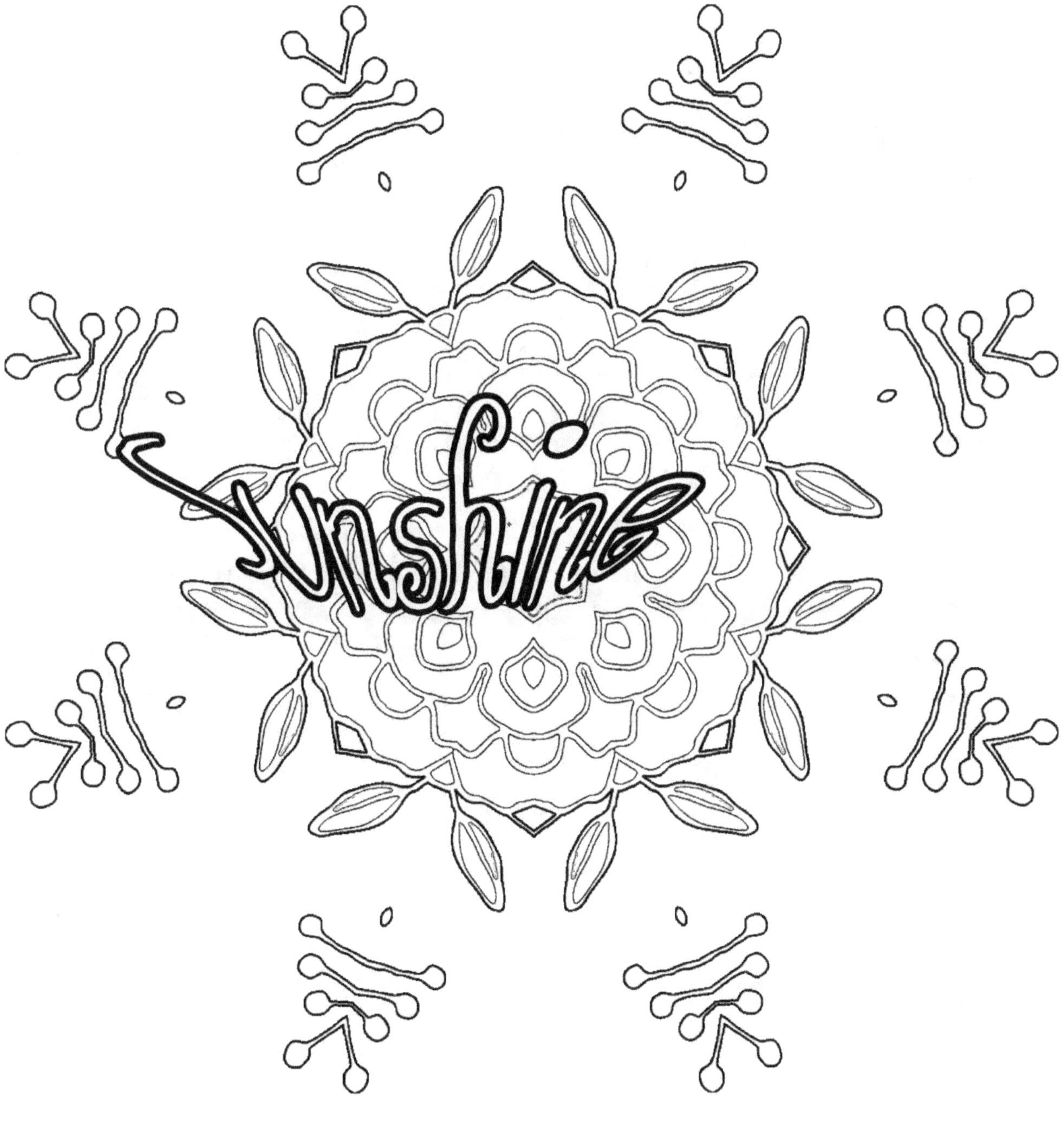
Sunshine

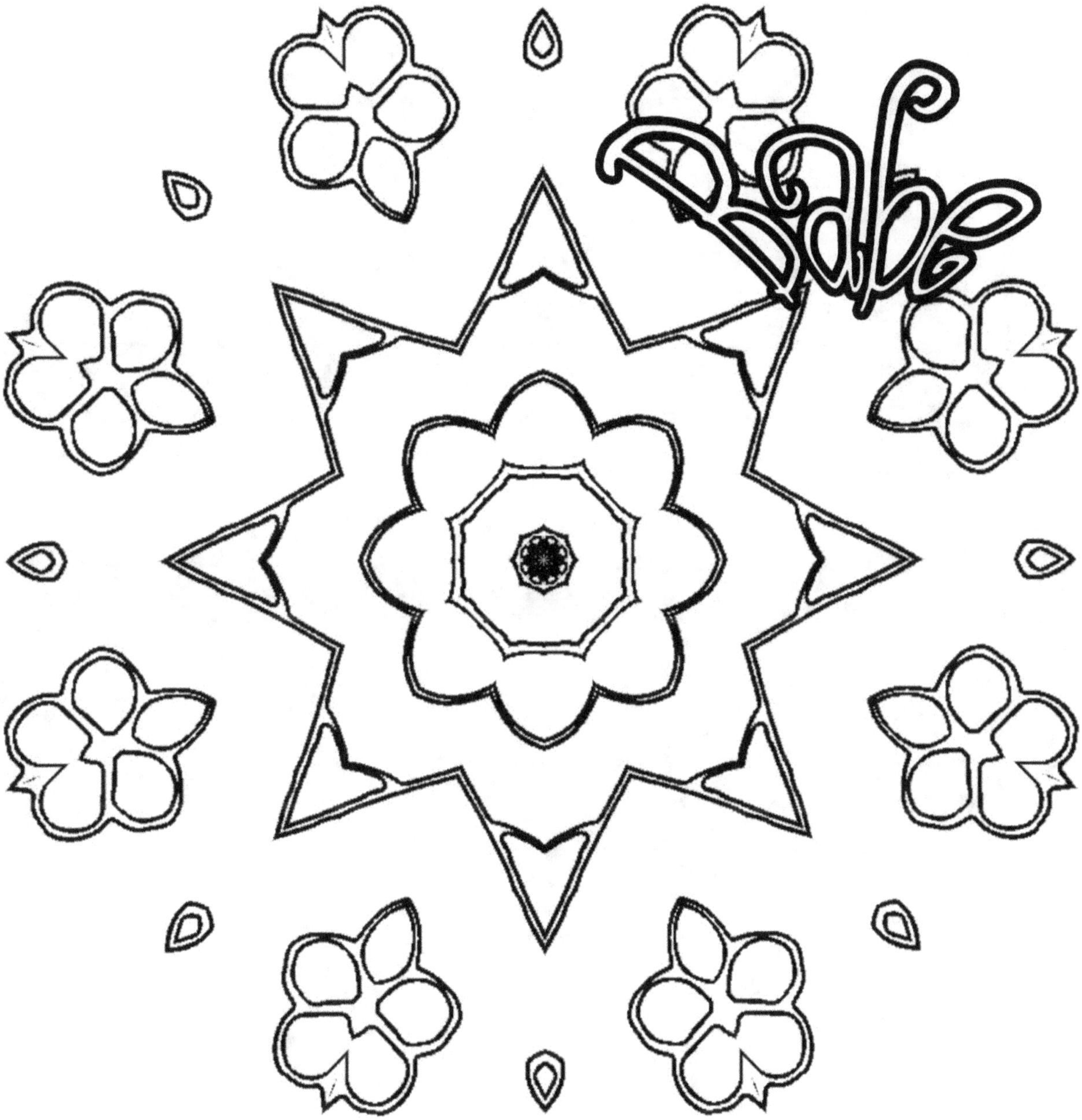
Babe

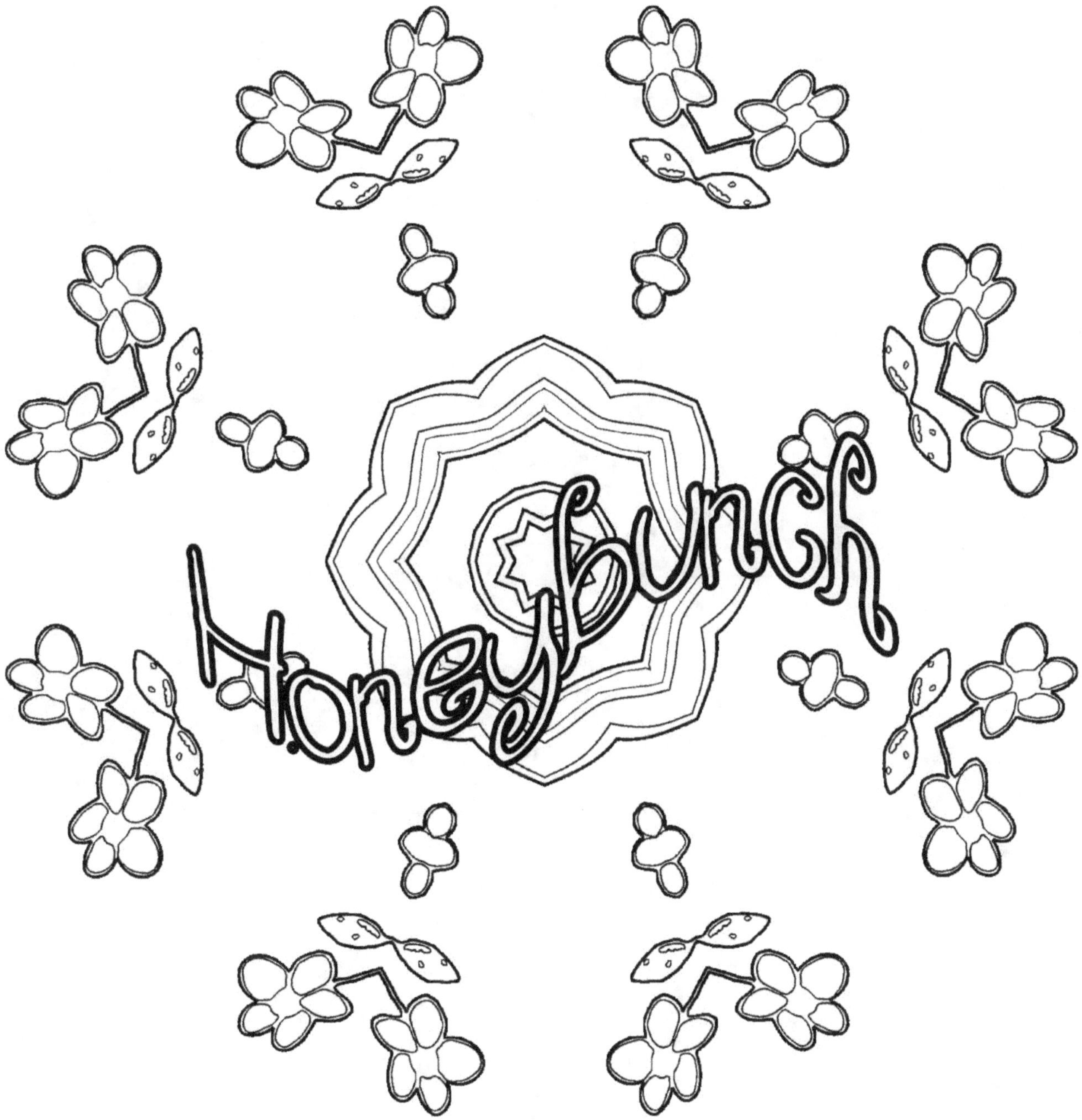
Honeybunch

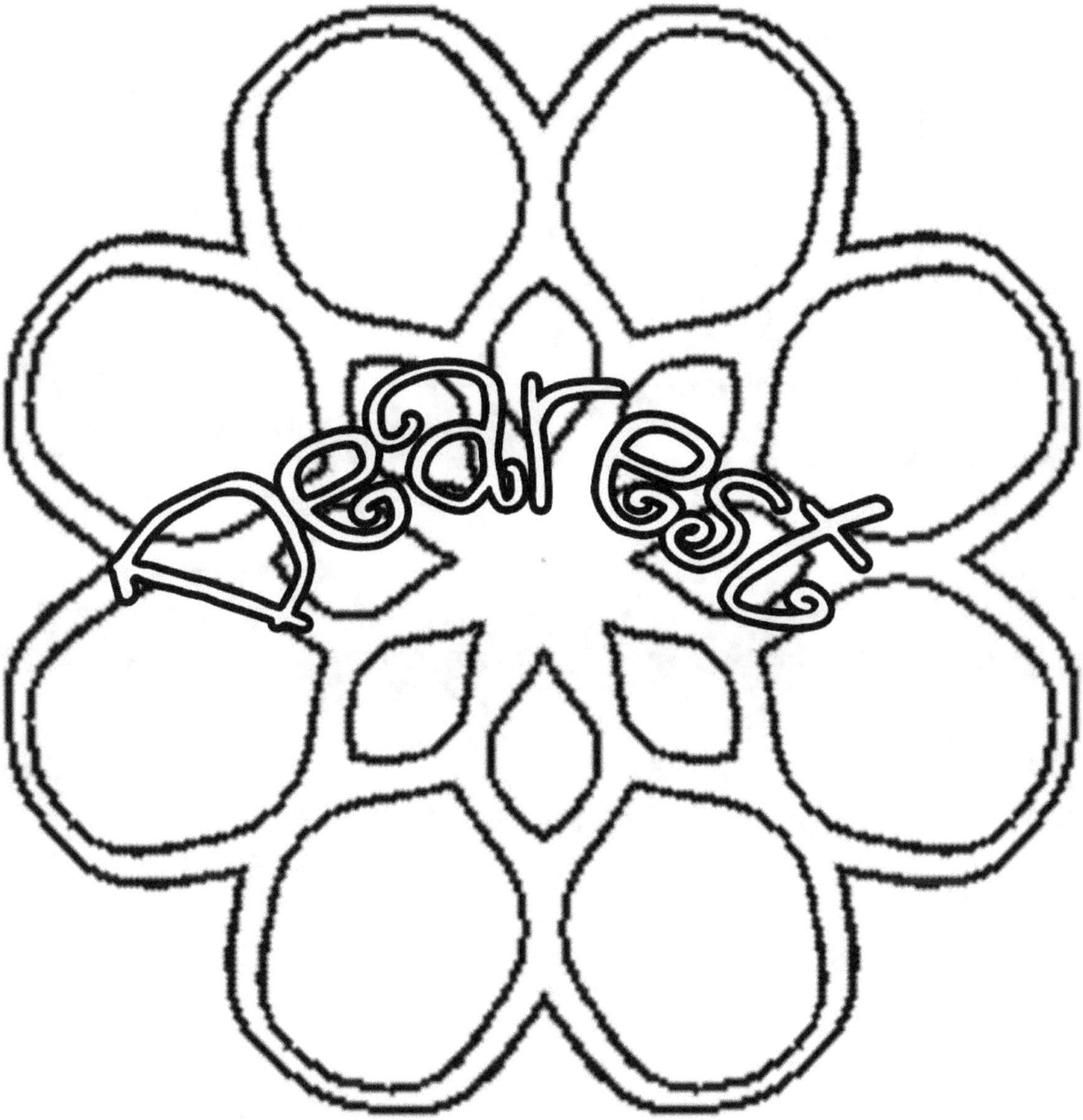
Dearest

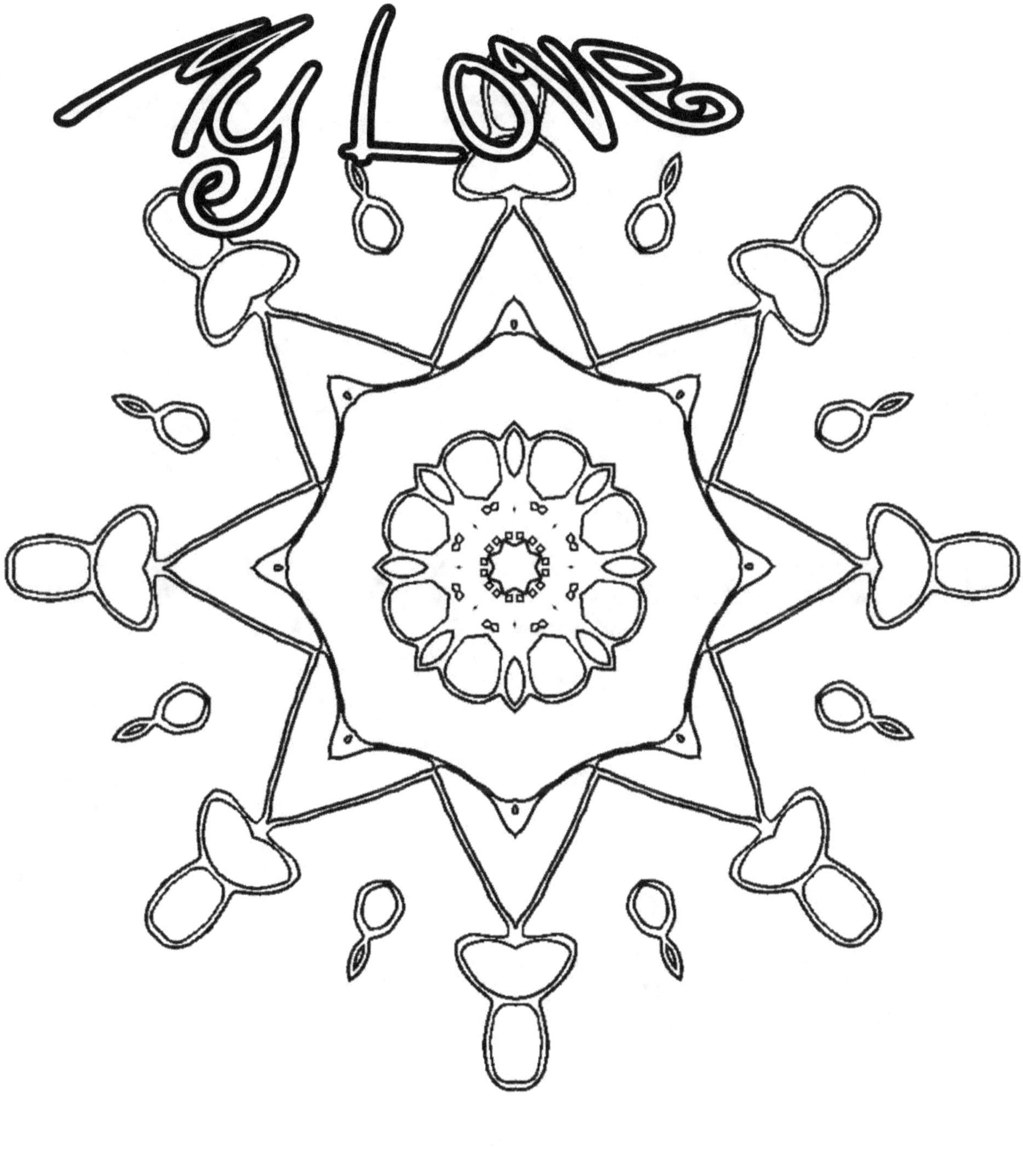
My Love

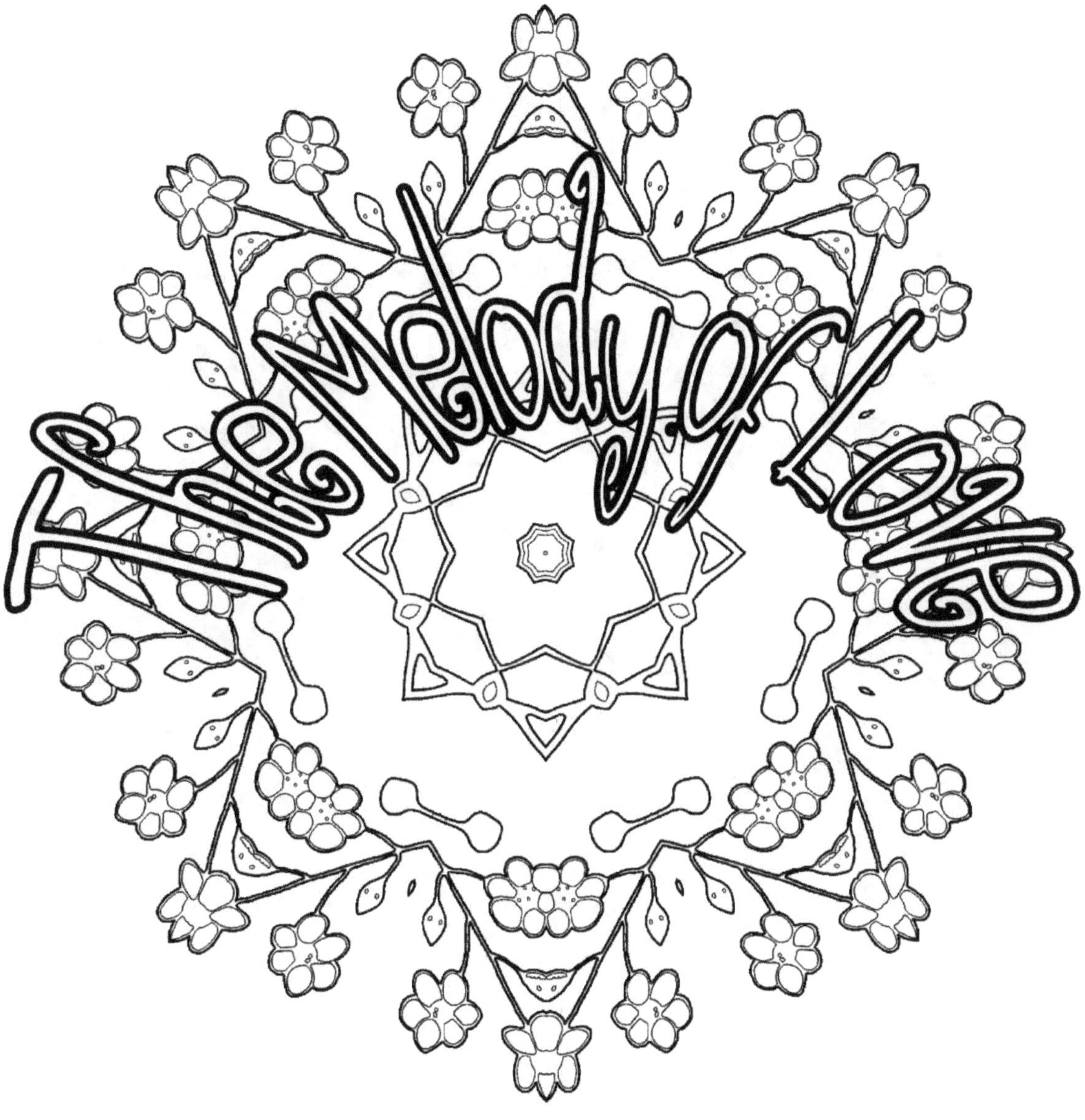
The Melody of Love

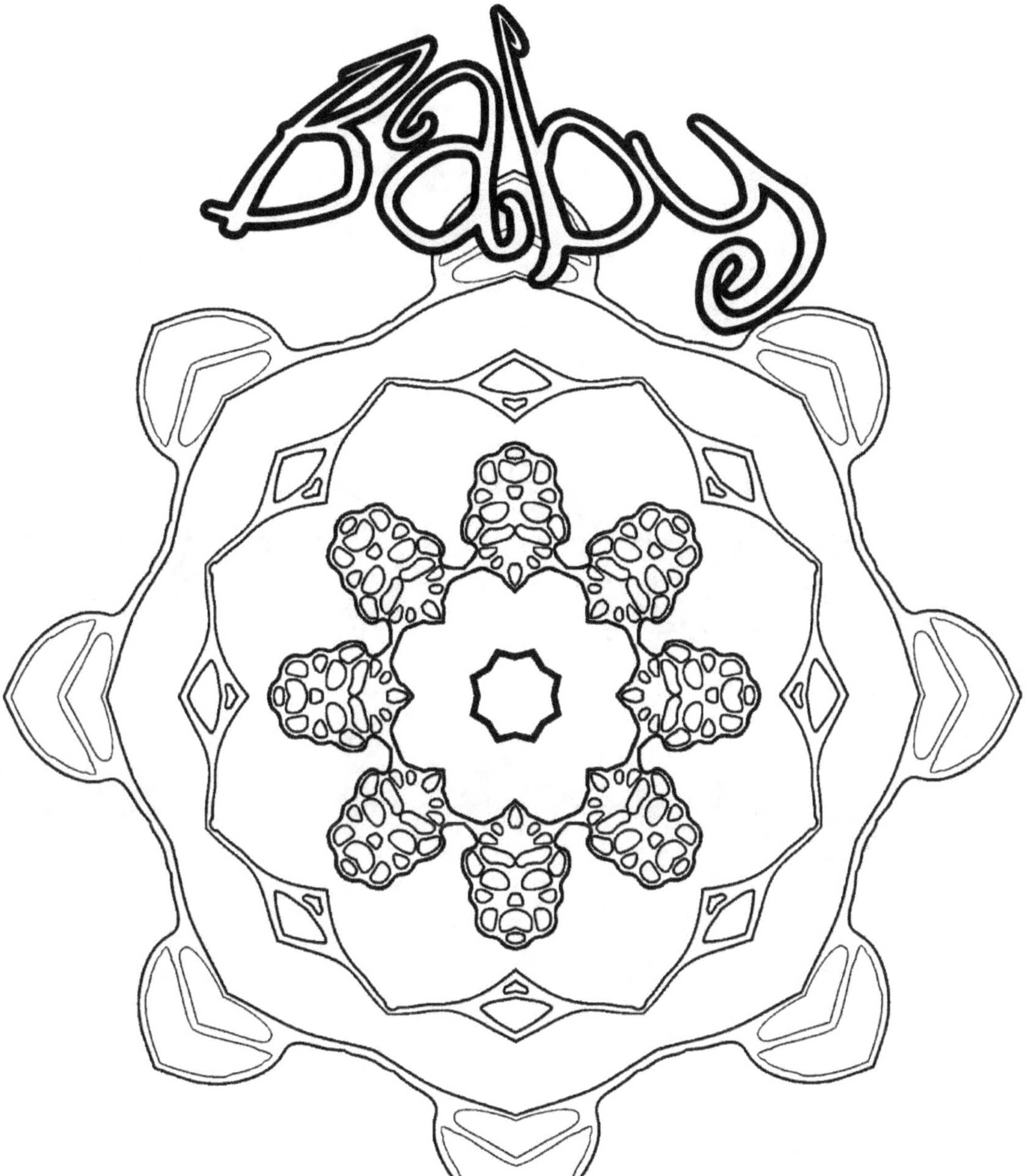
Baby

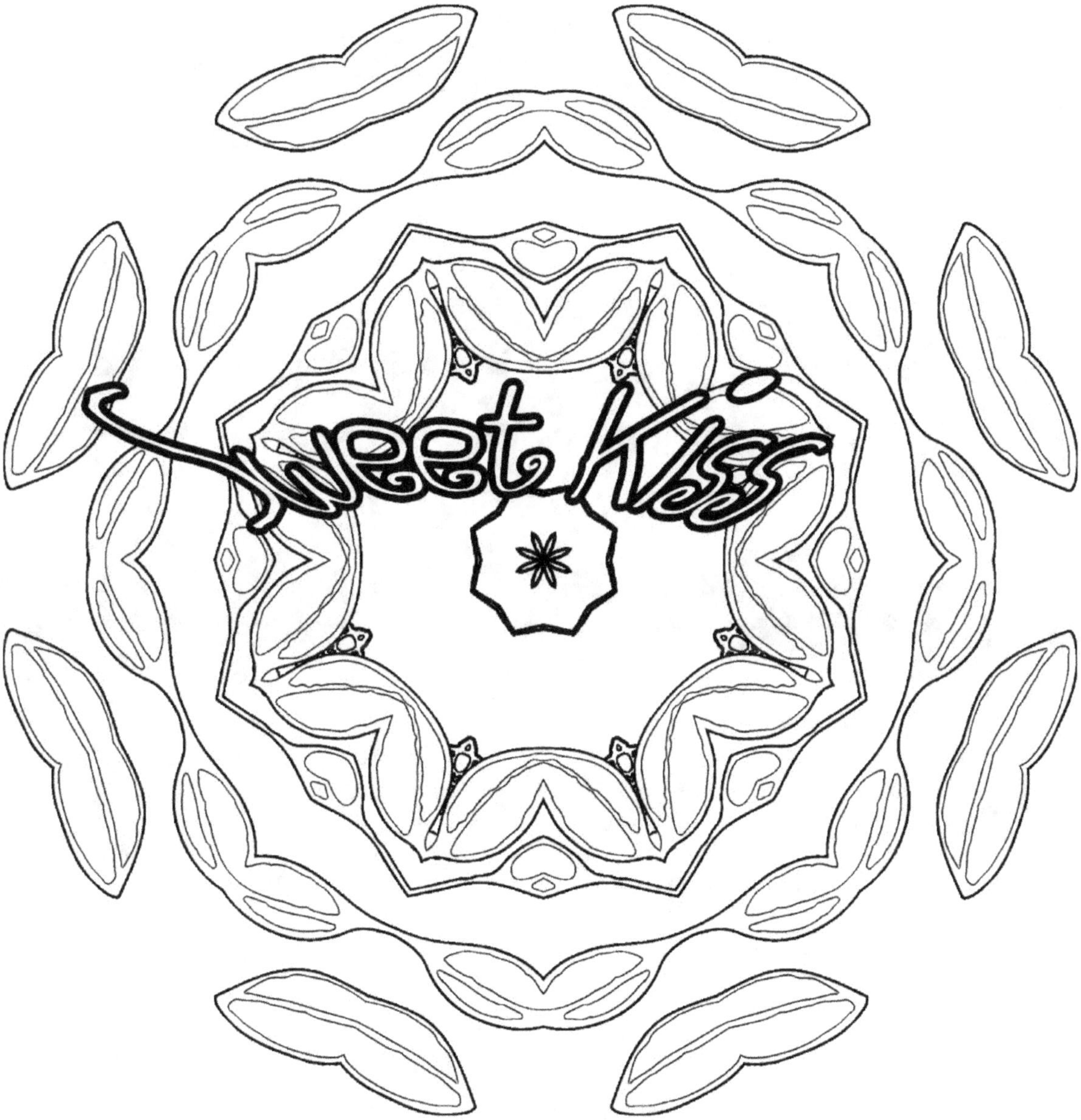
Sweet Kiss

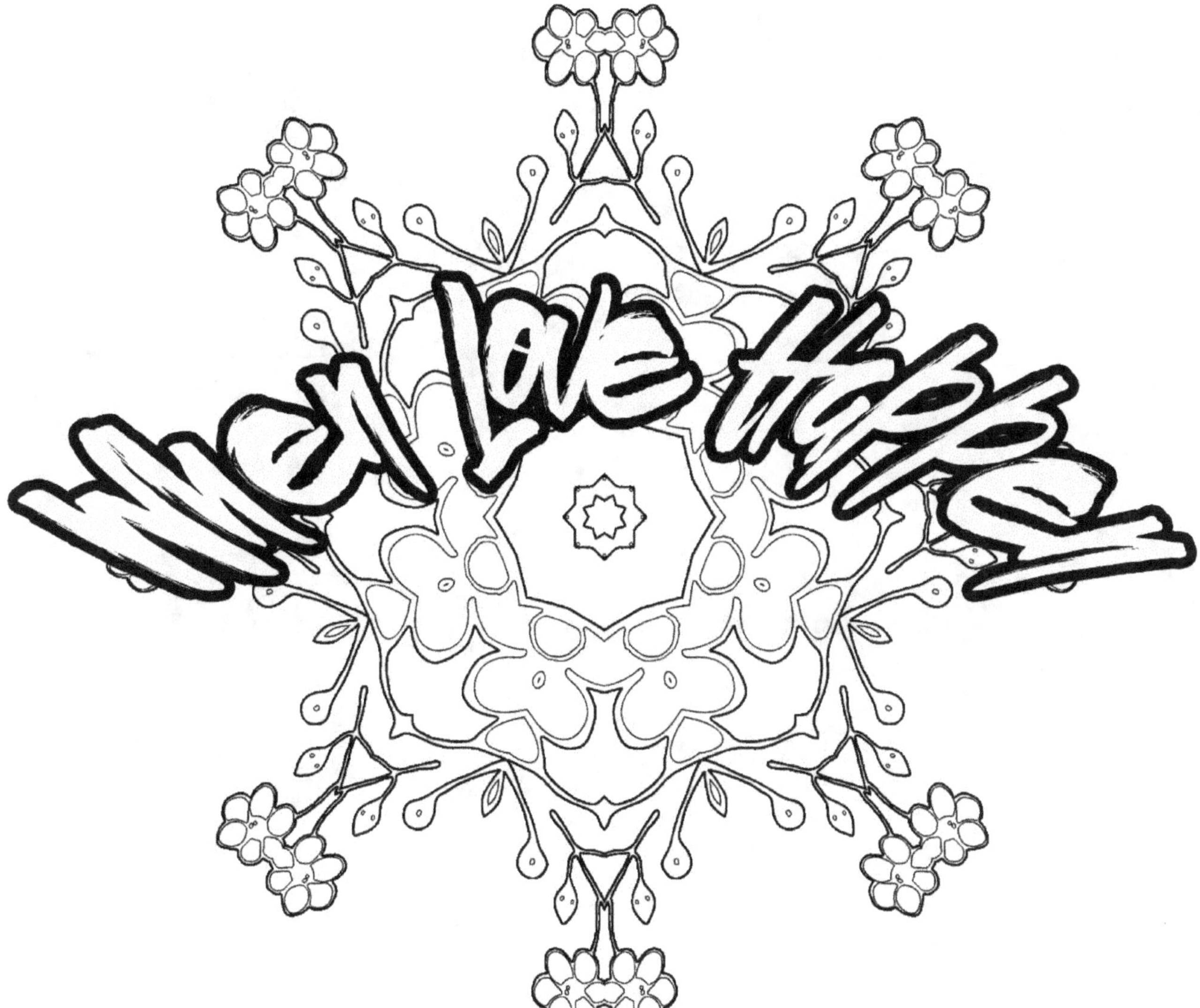
When Love Happens

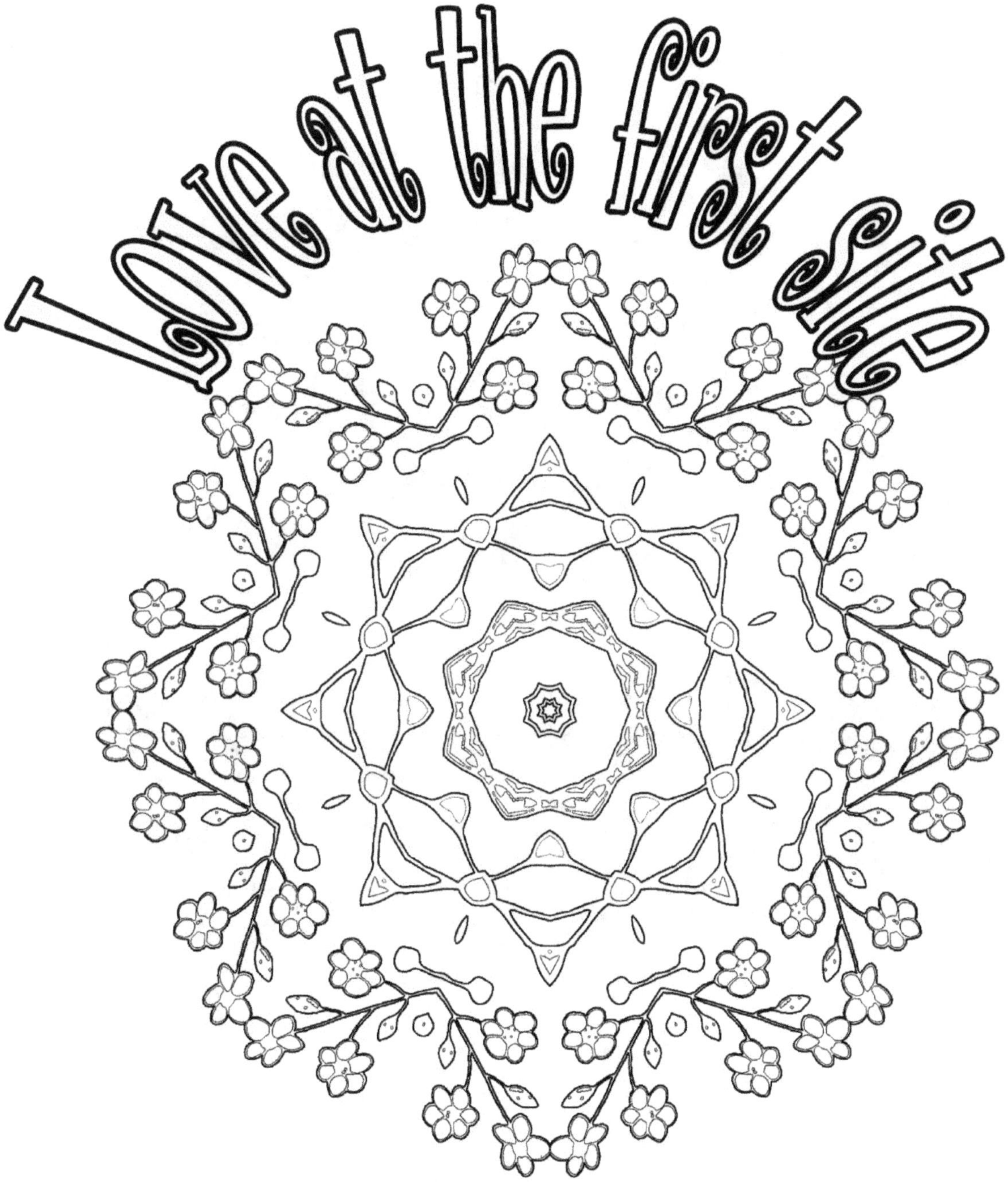
Love at the first site

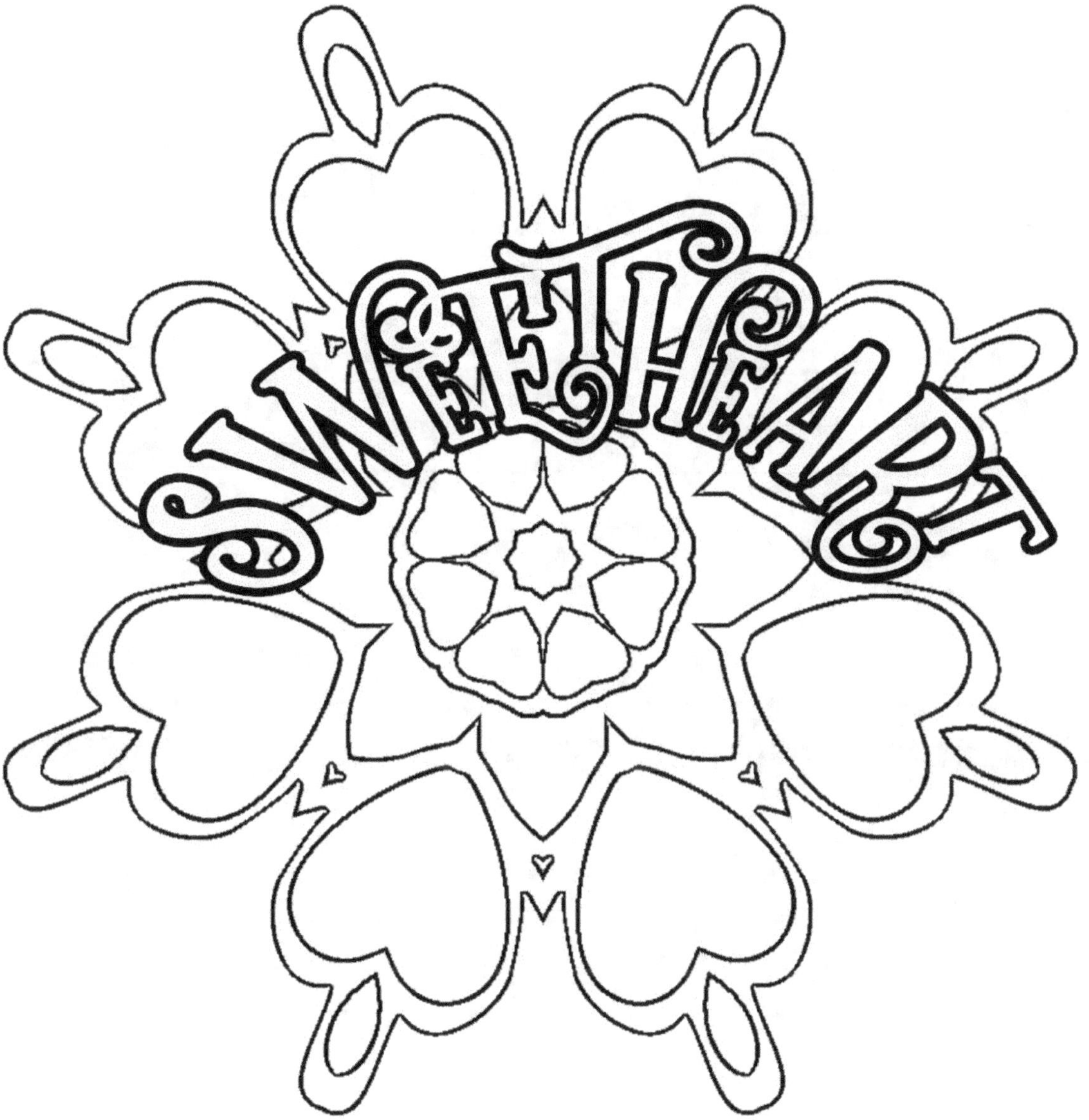
SWEETHEART

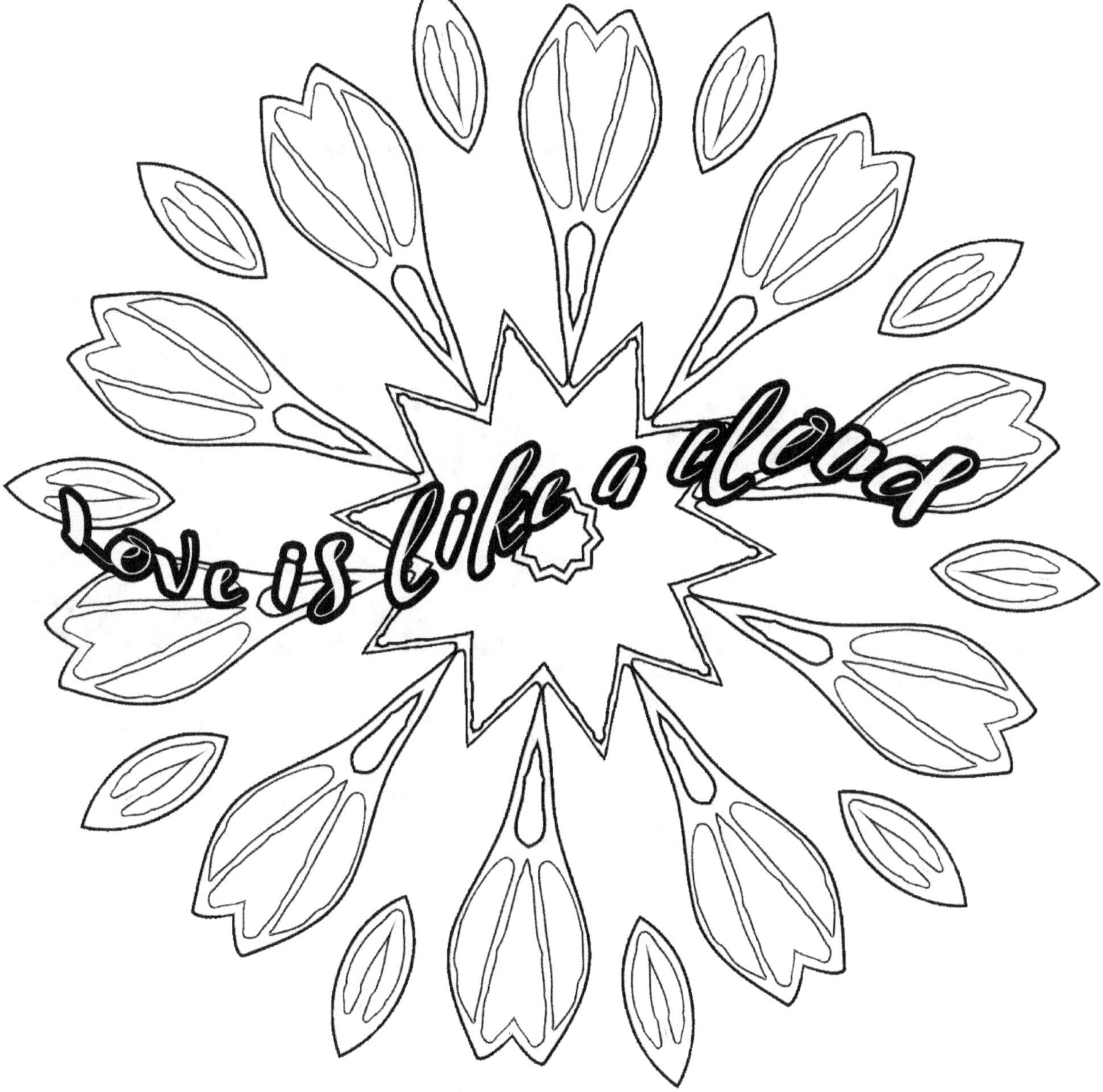
Love is like a cloud

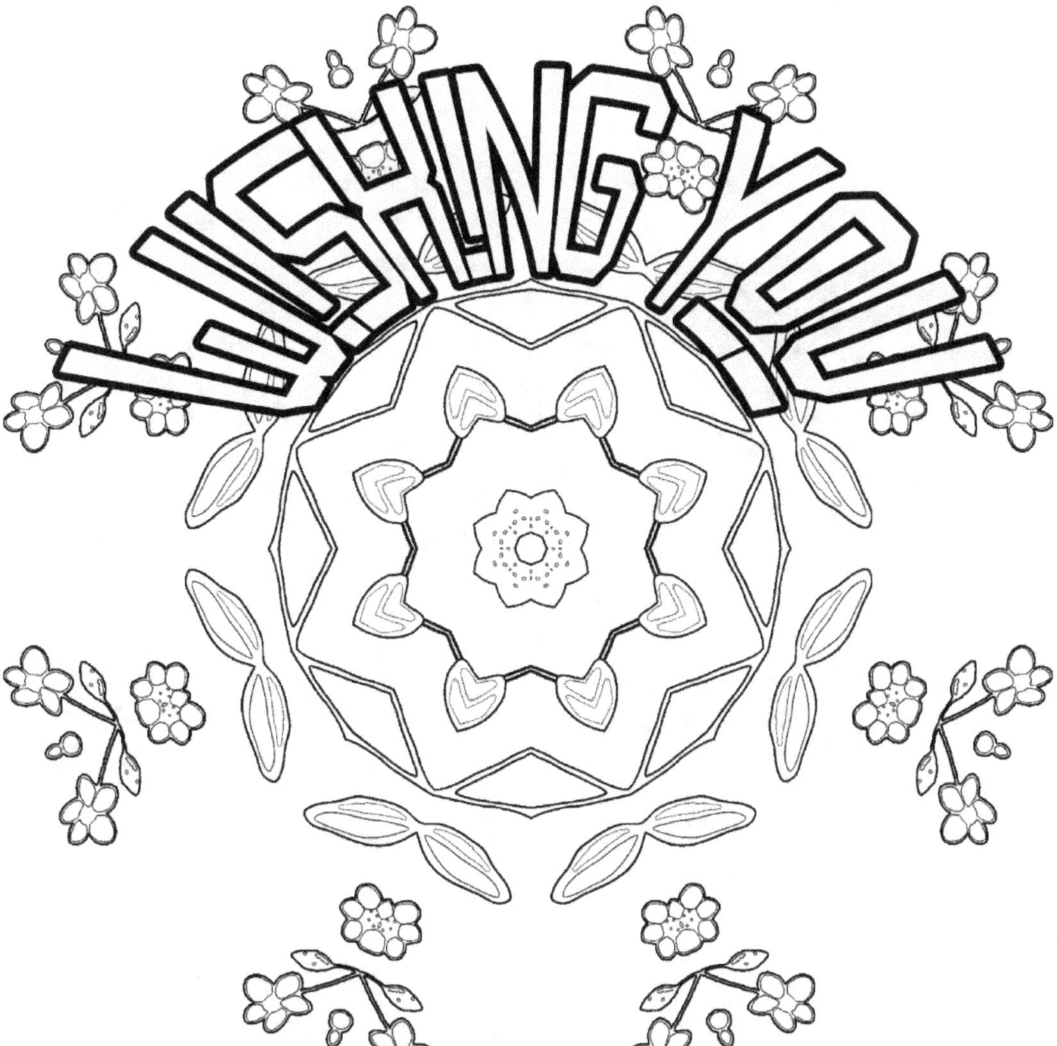
WISHING YOU

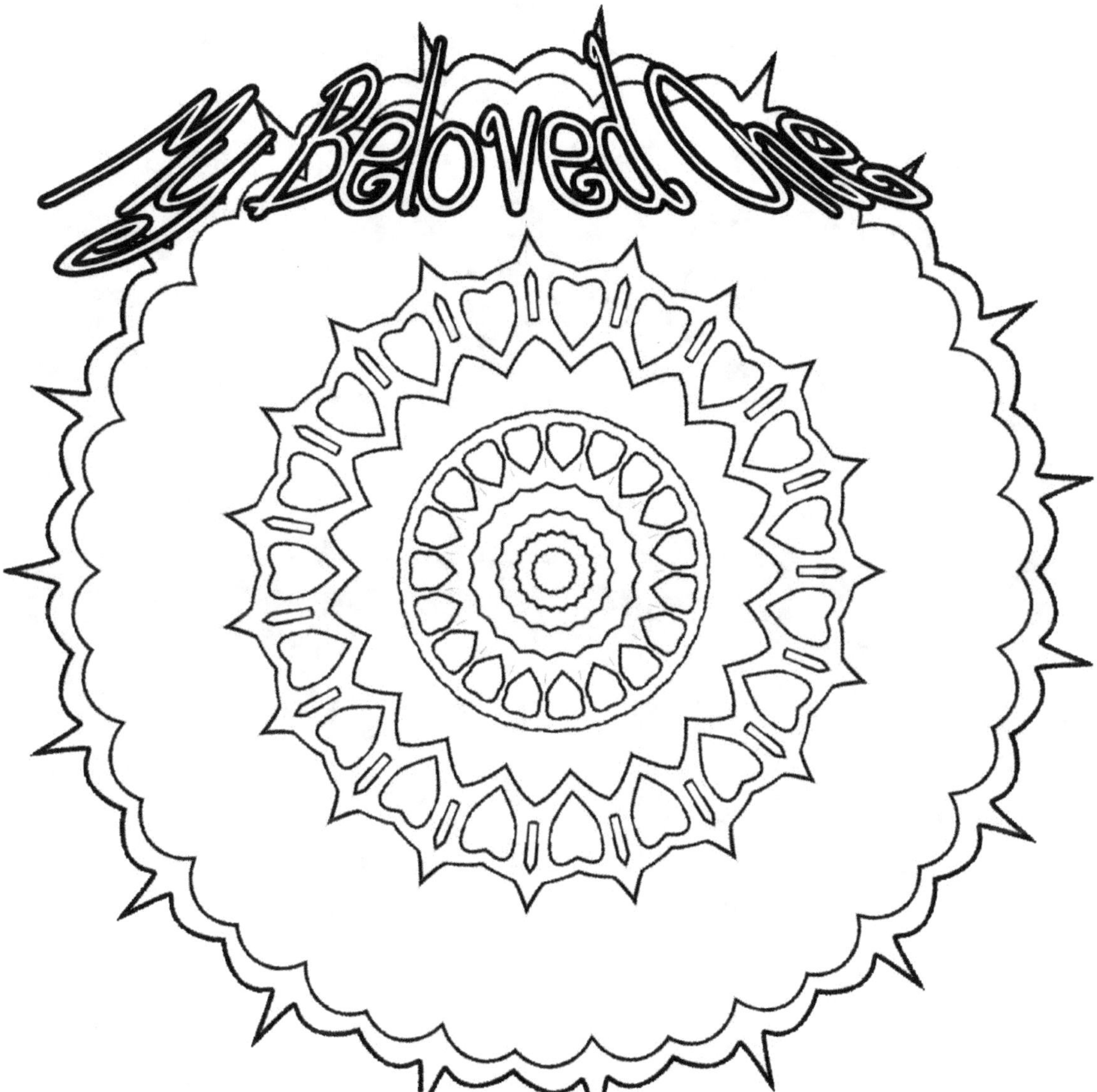
My Beloved One

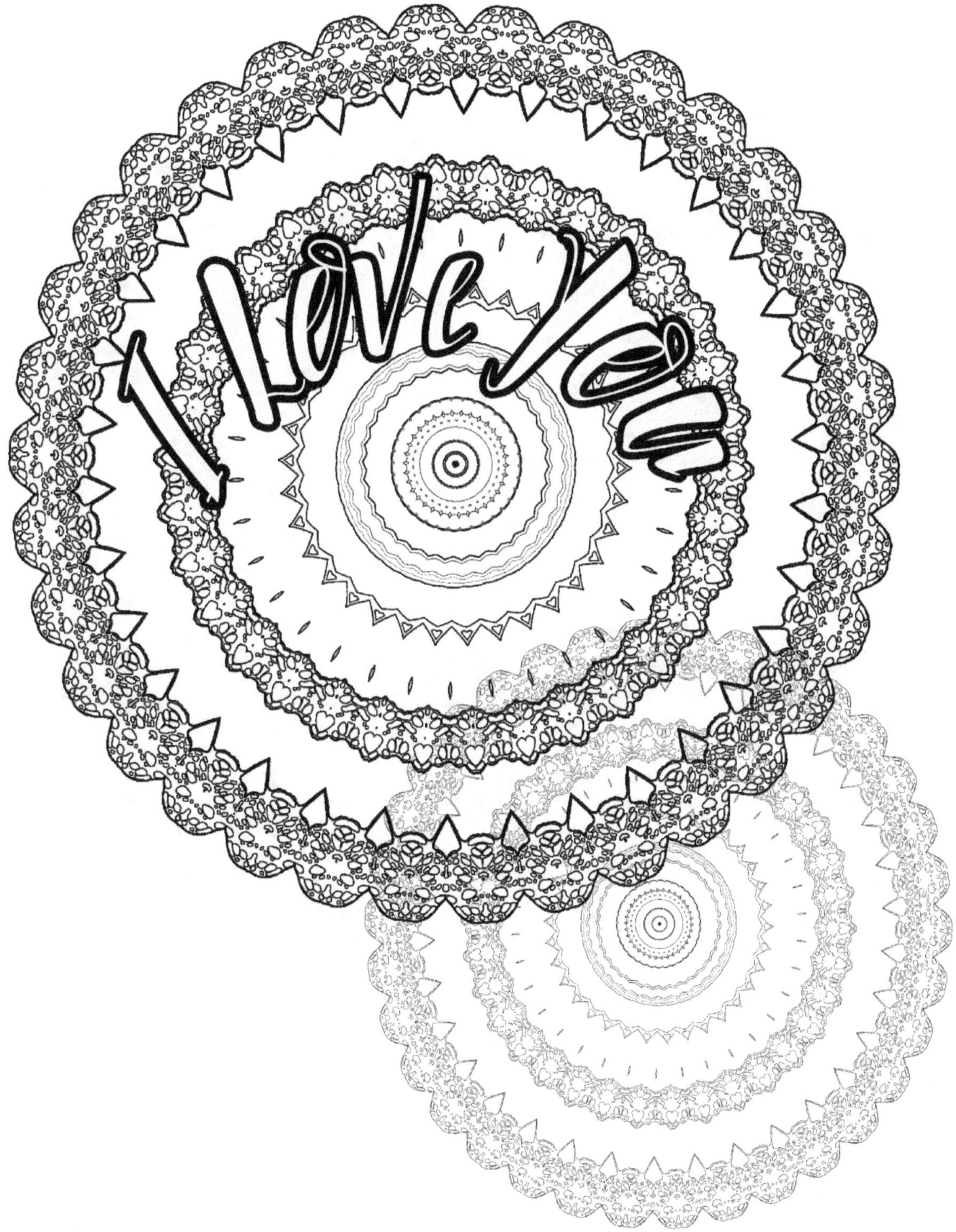
I Love You

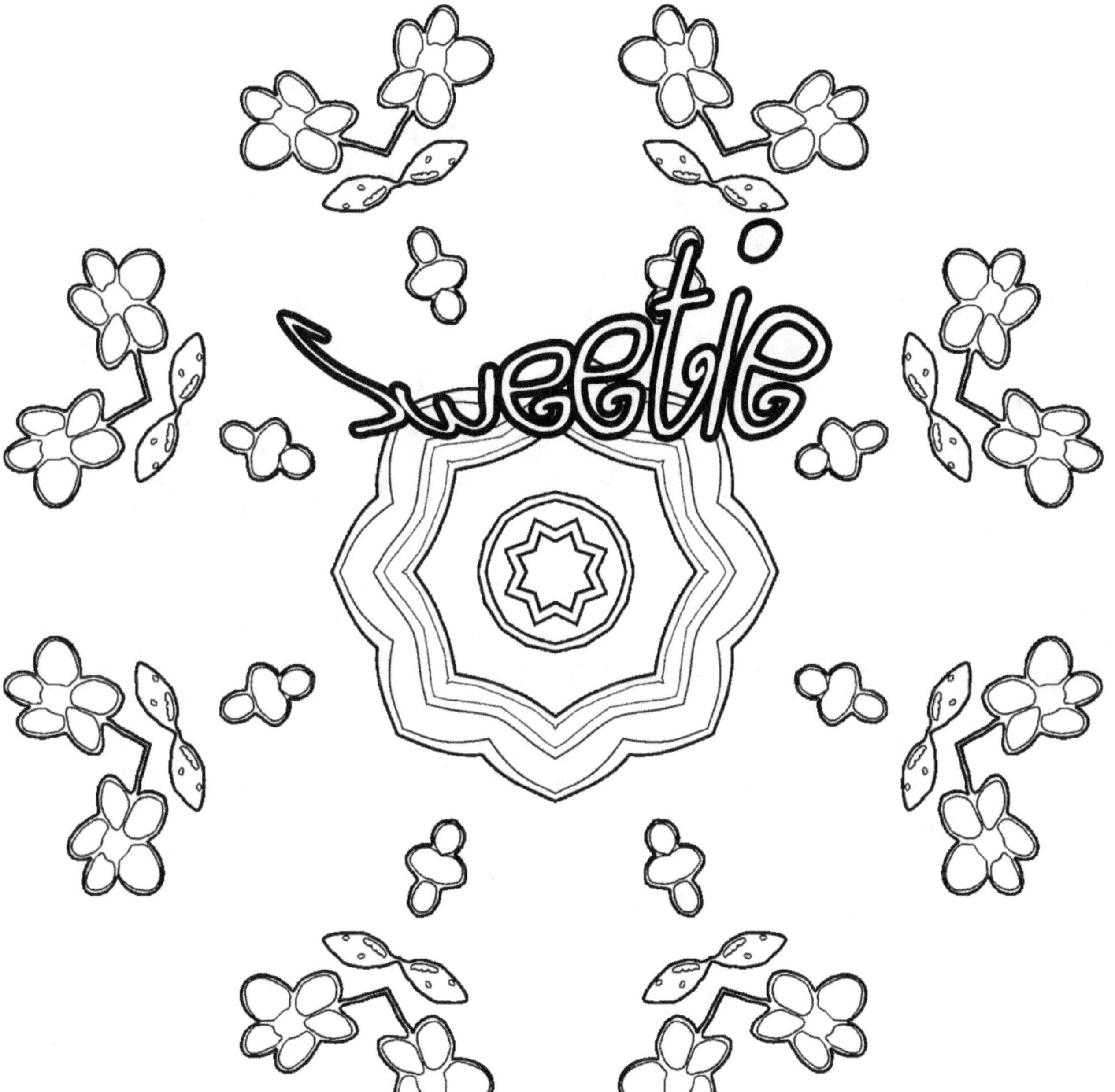
Sweetie

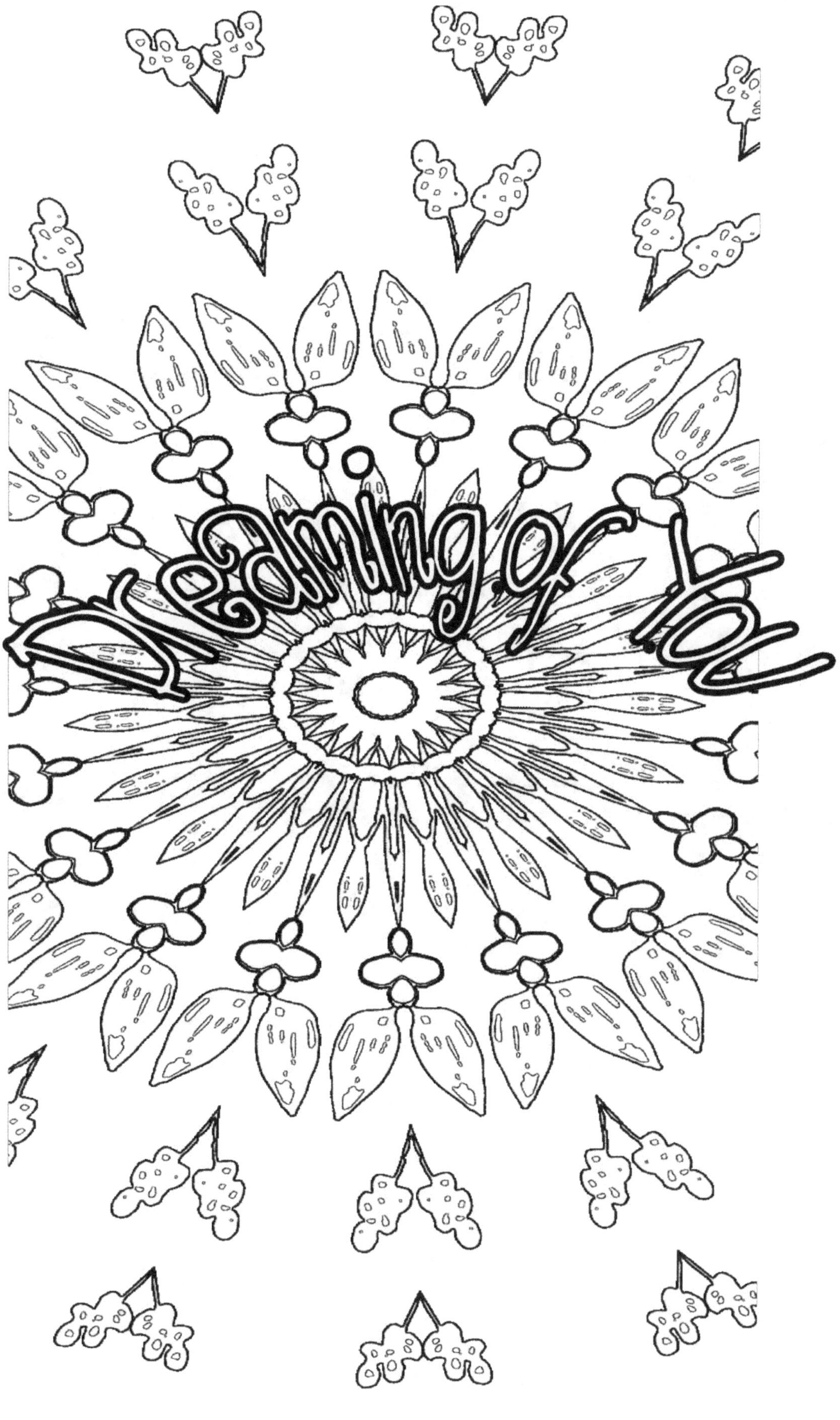
Dreaming of You

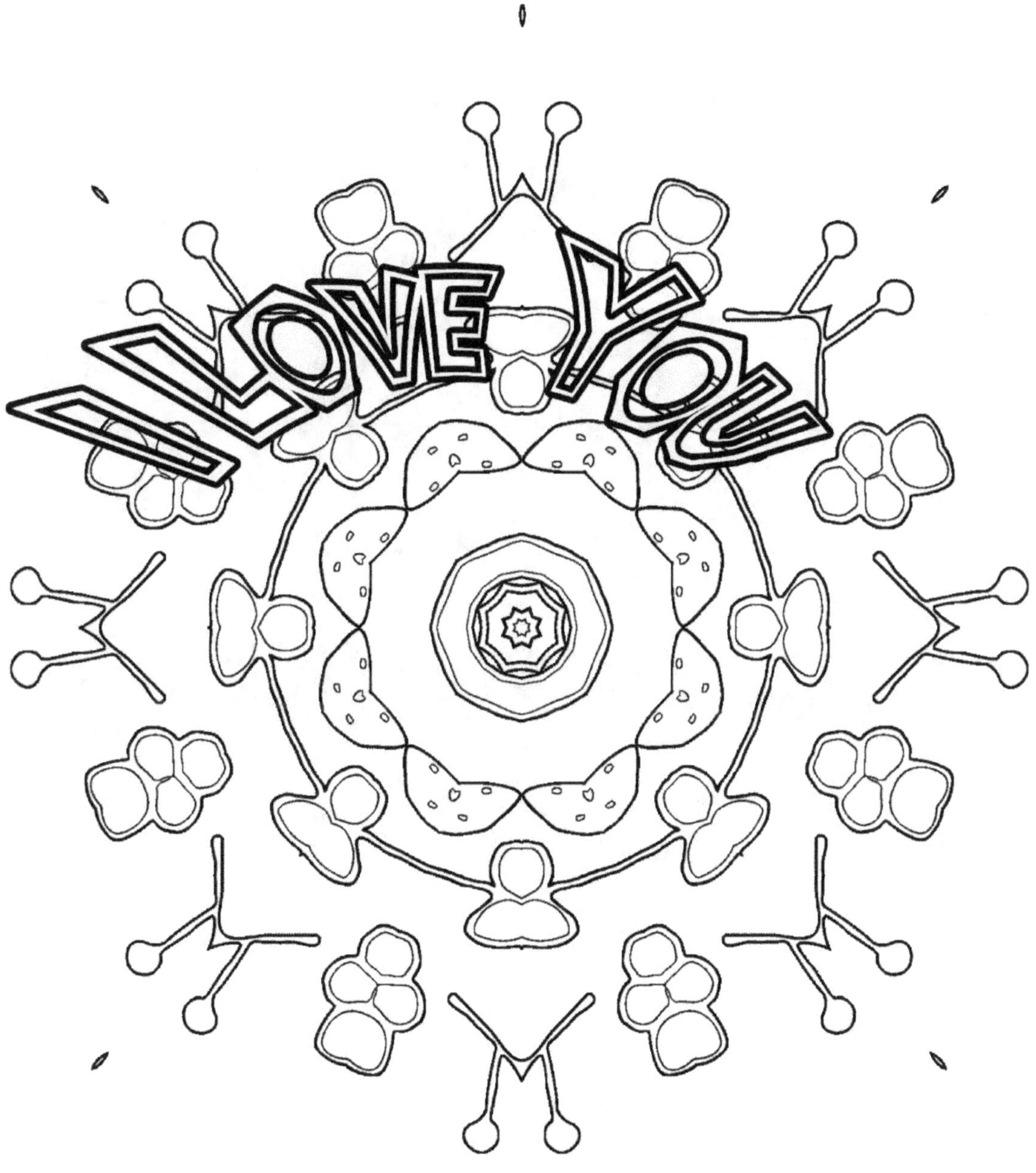
I LOVE YOU

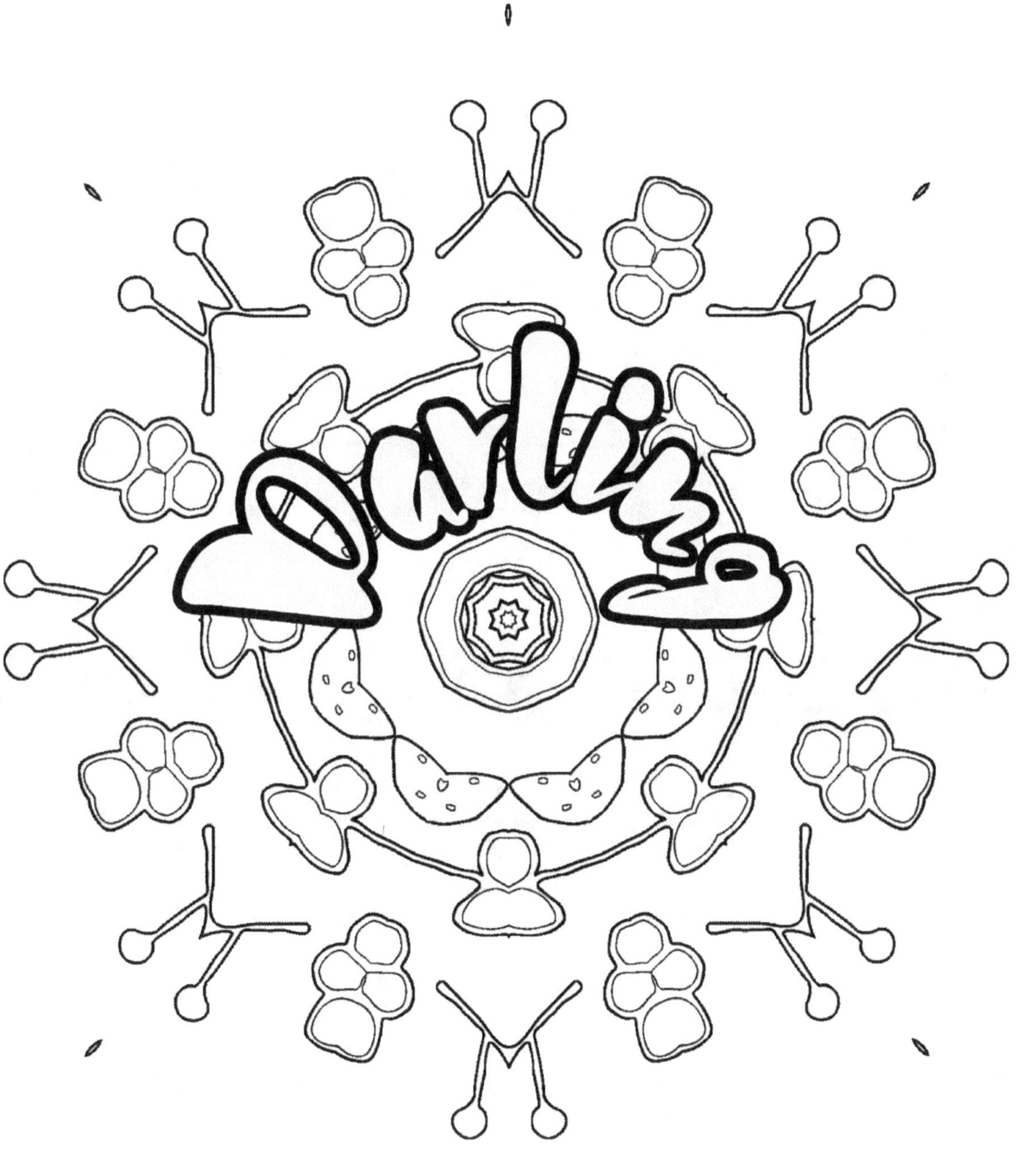
Darling

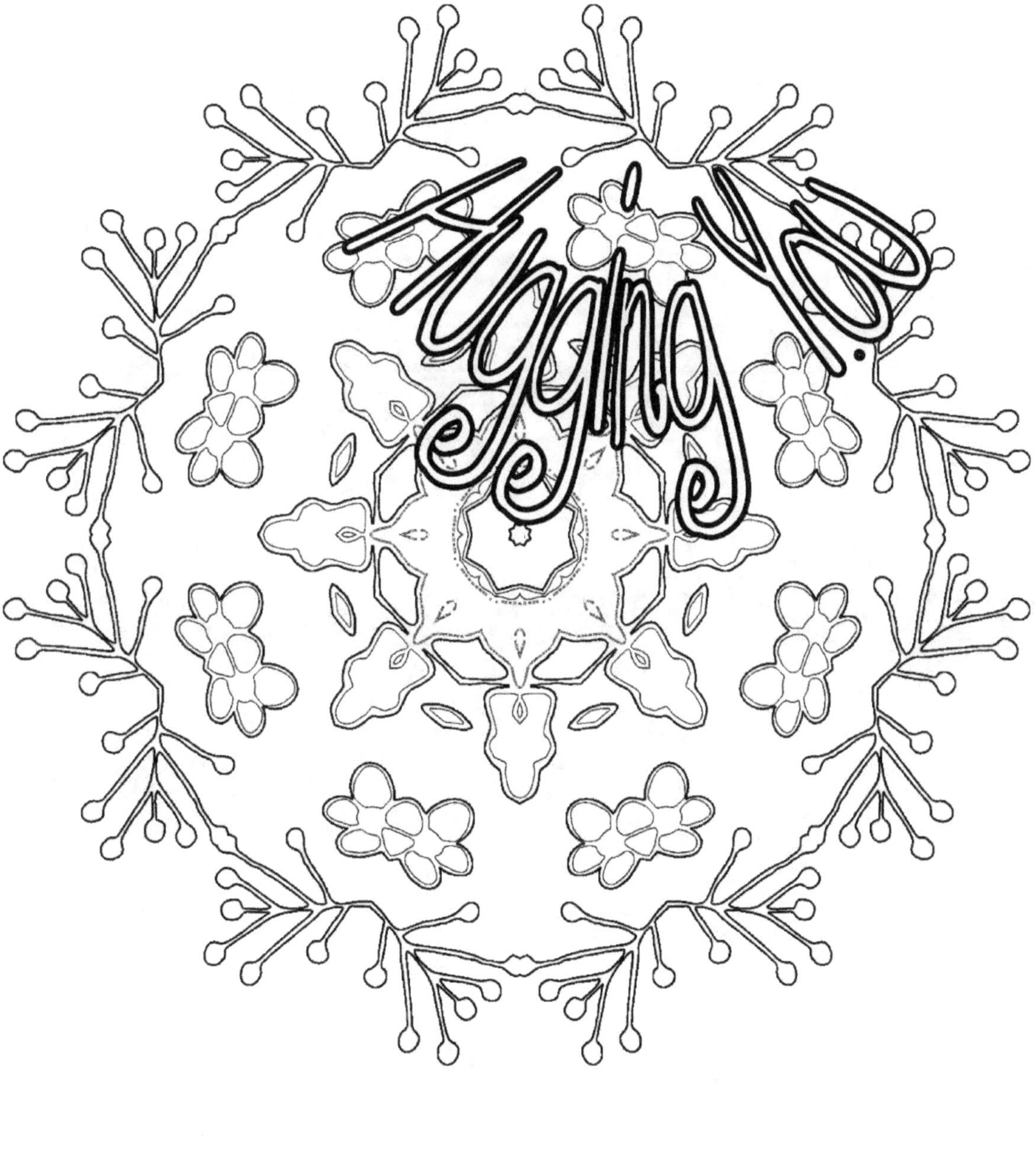
Hugging You

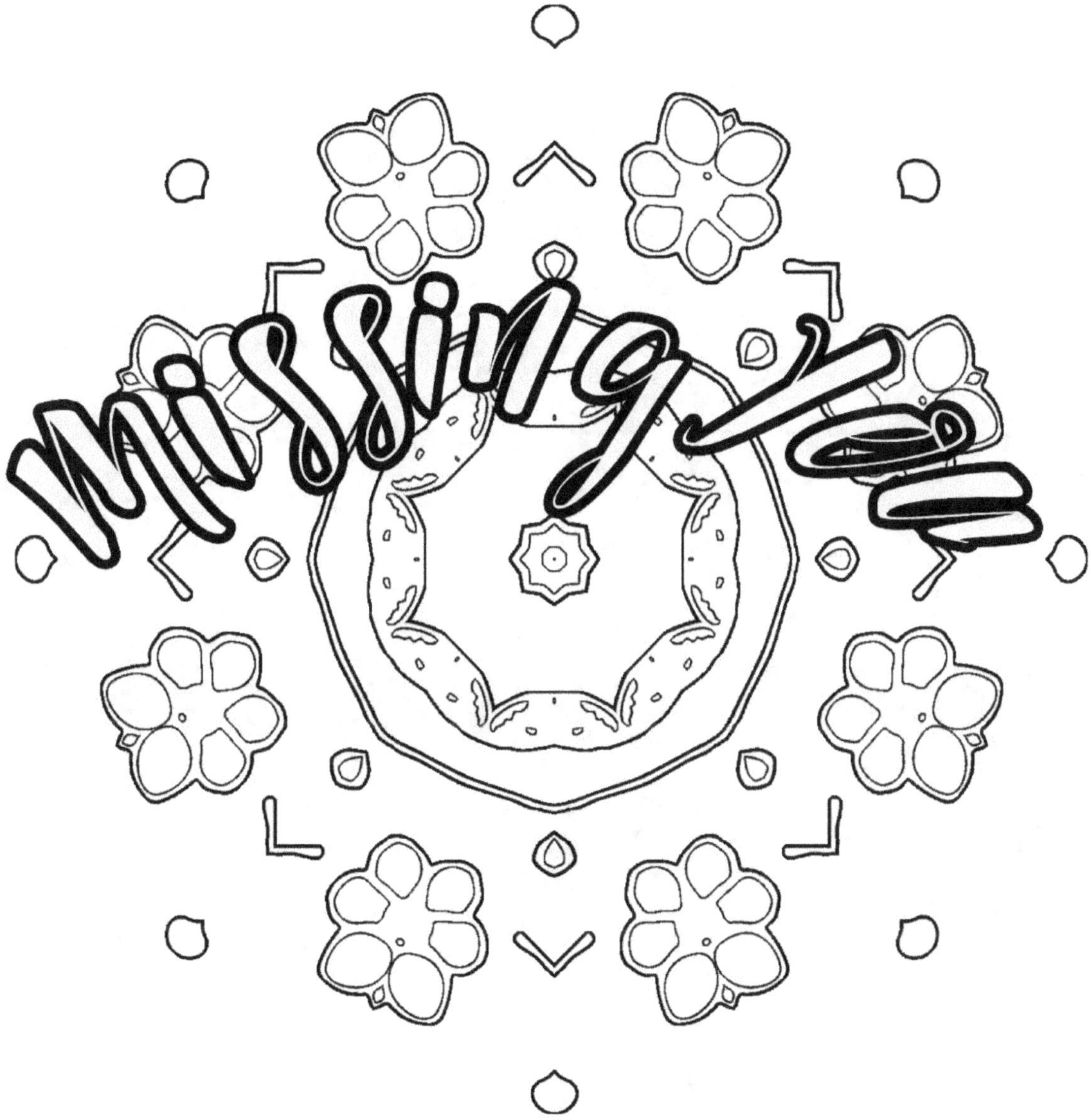
Missing You

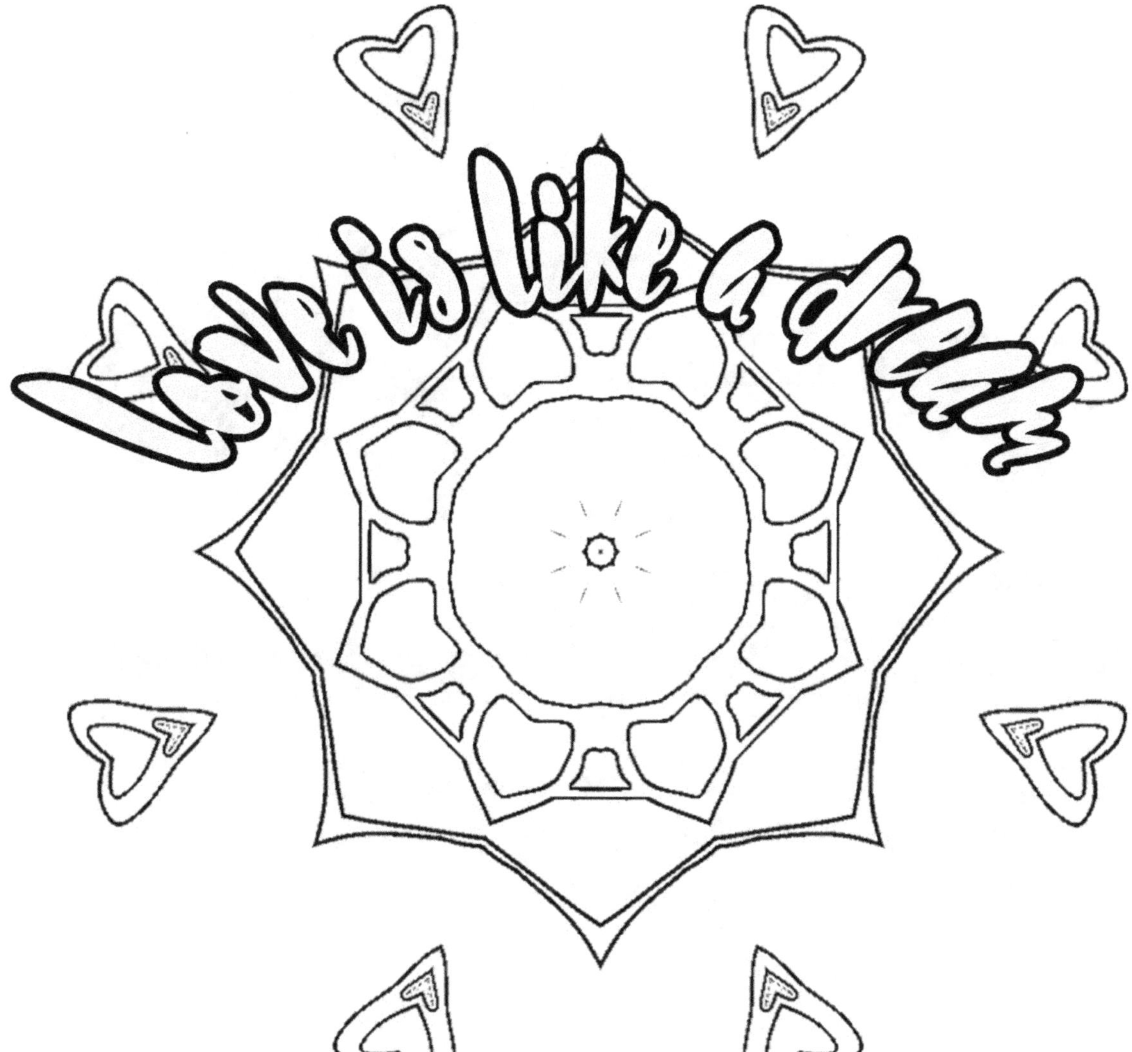
love is like a dream

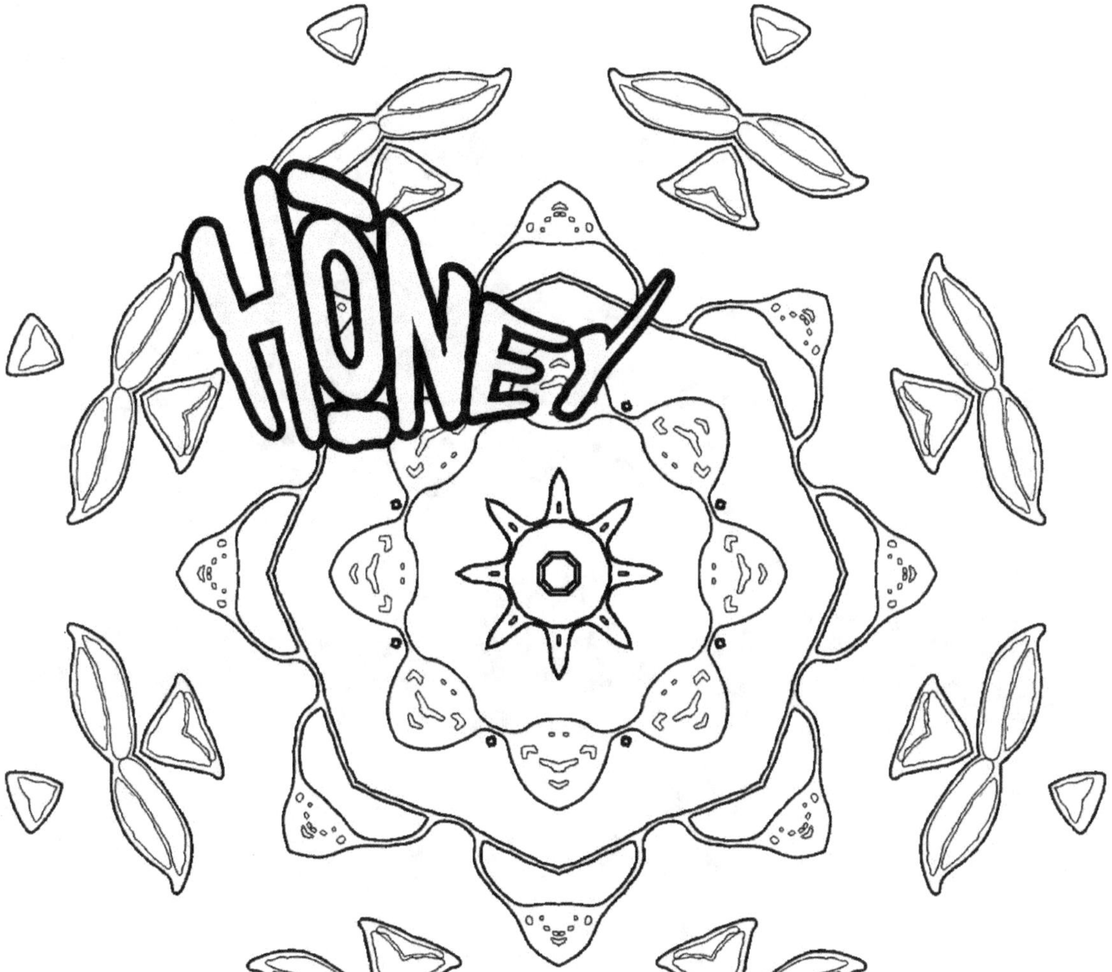
HONEY

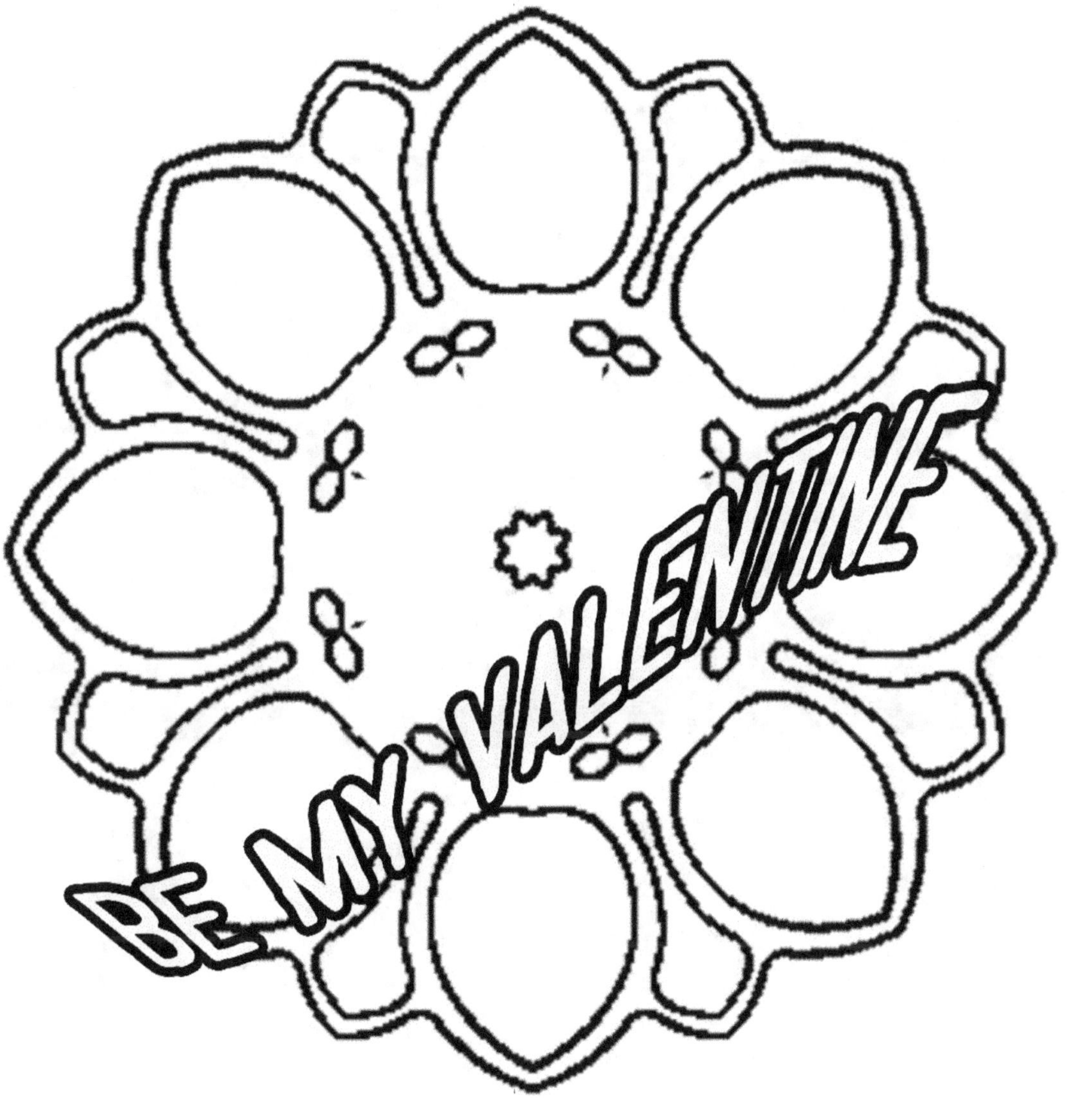
BE MY VALENITINE

www.ingramcontent.com/pod-product-compliance
Lightning Source LLC
Chambersburg PA
CBHW081748170526
45167CB00009B/3961
* 9 7 8 1 5 4 3 0 2 4 0 6 7 *